JUST IN CASE

Poems in My Pocket

CHARLOTTE MITCHELL

I heard this phrase,
'psycho-social support'—
Is this a new word for love?
I thought.

SOUVENIR PRESS

Also by Charlotte Mitchell

I WANT TO GO HOME
Poems Through a Day

First published 1991 by Souvenir Press Ltd,
43 Great Russell Street, London WC1B 3PA
and simultaneously in Canada

ISBN 0 285 630601

Photoset and printed in Great Britain by
Redwood Press Limited, Melksham, Wiltshire

CONTENTS

The Portfolio
or
The Actual Day of the Daughter's Interview for Art School

The daughter in charge of the portfolio,
barge mistress of the cargo,
turns like a tiger in tears, on the ratepayer,
the mother, 'Get OUT,
What do you know about mounting?'
Counting
her heartbeats the mother
becomes other-
wise engaged checking the hours still left
before the portfolio sets forth
for an emporium of Art Instruction
in the North.

The knowledge she has stored from her youth
she has not proffered to her daughter,
offered to
this tiger who guards and detests her portfolio,
who stumps
from room to room and hates her hair,
who lumps
enormous cardboard walls and *papier mâché* heads
and hates her hair,
and calls obscenities to art schools everywhere.

'What am I going to art school FOR? I won't get in.'

'I can't get in
to a single room without falling over,'
the mother observes,
'just look at this place!'
'OH,' the tiger replies,
be like that! I hate it when you make that face.'
The mother crouches in the kitchen
amongst the other rejections,
the watercolours, collages given the push,
scrumped around the rubbish bin.
And then the tiger's din
again —
'This portfolio is ridiculous,' comes the frantic call,
as it spreads and bulges leaking
photos, pastels, charcoals, oils,
the narrow hall
stretched to contain it.
The tapes burst, the knots hang useless
as it opens up.

Avoiding the bloodcurdling shriek from the top stair
the mother, with one mighty leap,
makes for the front door and fresher air —
A shadow rises behind the frosted glass.
'Taxi, Madam?'
Waving dumbly into the house
at the tiger still in her nightie over the spilt load
the mother beats it down the road.

'He looked like a man with a stout heart,
he looked quite sweet,'
the mother comforts her retreating feet.

Later in the day she meets Stout Heart leaning on his
    minicab,
a knight, a Galahad, a blade.
'Get her to King's Cross all right?'
she asks, afraid.
'Oh yes, no problem,
plenty of time — train was delayed,
carried that cardboard thing to the train for her,
bit of a dodgy affair,' Stout Heart replies
without, apparently, a care.

In the kitchen alone, later,
with the debris, the ink and the Letraset,
stalks of photo edges criss-crossing the carpet,
and don't forget the mountains of clothes and shoes
that were not in the end
allowed to go North to be considered for an Art BA.
The actual night of the actual day of the famous
    interview,
a note in black marker from the daughter, peeps from the
    mess:
'Thanks for everything, Ma,'
— Ah —

Whereat the mother
takes charge
of her own portfolio,
her face,
the one she's lumped about everywhere,
since she was born,
and lets out the breath she's been hanging onto fiercely
since dawn.

Rose Pringle

How we talked, how we laughed,
my sister and I
finding gaps in each other's recall . . .
'Can't you remember Rose Pringle?
'Can't you remember at all?'
'No, I can't remember Rose Pringle.'
'Well, she took me and you
to lunch and the zoo
and you got upset,
how could you forget?'

'Darling,' I said, 'how old was I then?'
'You were three,' said my sister, 'and I was ten.
But, she was a little bit stern with us,
and the lunch place was just a bit grand for you.'

'Did I make a terrible fuss?'

'No, not too much fuss,' said my sister,
generous to a fault.
'You were only little, only three . . .'
But I bet I screamed and screamed, I thought,
knowing me.

The Wardrobe

My friend had this wardrobe stuck in her narrow hall
waiting for an offspring to come and fetch it.
Squeezing past it into the kitchen, I observed cheerfully,
'It'll be so good when it's gone,
the hall will seem bigger than before,
it will be exciting.'

A few days later I had reason to call
and found an empty hall,
free and commodious.

'There you are,' I said, 'it was worth
having a wardrobe in it for a month or two,
you can appreciate it now, the space, the hall,
you can skip down it, we both can skip down it — '

But as I enjoyed myself, I clocked the wardrobe
skulking in the middle of the sitting-room,
taking up a different space . . .
I nearly began my little philosophy again,
but it wasn't going to work a second time,
not when I saw
my friend's dark wardrobe-ridden face.

Fashion

'May I ask something?' I said, meek,
to the girl in the overheated, spotlit boutique,
Who was folding a fluffy, purple, sparkle-ridden top.
'Do you do a larger size than fourteen?'
'Oh, no,' she replied, 'this is a fashion shop.'

'So,' I said, darkly, 'is that it?'
Do I just keep quiet, then,
and go on a diet?
Or are the makers of these tea-towel narrow skirts
in business with the makers
of low calorie desserts?

Not for the Uncertain

I went to this party at this posh tall house
with stripped, shiny floor boards
squeaky and cold,
rugs pale and virginal,
and all was still and new,
nothing looked old.
Cream and grey and black and brown,
and I laid my shabby coat on a king-sized duvet
plump with goose-feather down.
It was all right for certain people
but not for the uncertain.
I went to this party at this posh tall house
with a laboratory instead of a kitchen,
and long low sofas and squat low chairs
and no help for my neck to rest my head,
and nowhere to smash a plate
and nowhere to hurl tomato sauce
and no tomato sauce naturally
and nowhere to slam jam
on a piece of bread,
and nothing the least bit emotional being said.
I went to this party at this posh tall house
full of murmuring
and delicate clinking
of delicate drinking,
and paper-thin nourishment
in little porcelain bowls

and nowhere for a messy thought
to settle.
I wanted to cry
but I didn't, did I?
I aired a great deal of rubbish
and my champers went for a burton.
It was all right for certain people
but not for the uncertain.

A Little Less of Everything

In a café in Soho I overheard this man saying:
'Everyone should have a little less of everything
except, of course, those who've got less
than a little less of everything.'

'Oh,' said his companion, bending forward,
'it's too late for that; everyone wants everything
   nowadays,
the consumer society is extending to tribes, deserts,
jungles, whatever, if you like.'

'I don't like,' said the first man, 'all I'm saying
is that everyone should have a little less of everything
except of course those who've already got a little less
of everything.
Excess is corrupting.'
'Who are you to decide that?' said the second man
interrupting.
'I'm not deciding,' said the first man,
'it's just a plan of mine to get rid of things
and make some space, some space apart.'

But the second man's pager fastened to his heart
bleeped into the conversation
and he rushed off to keep another appointment.

A Levels

They sweated
blood,
young Josephine and Jane,
a flood
of tears
and History pain.
They bunked
off games
to cram in bulk
to entertain
a Shakespeare sulk.
   aching
   to get a few
   A levels
   together
   or rather
   their father
   ached
   wondering whether . . .
'What if they don't?' he said, and swooned,
a frown between his eyebrows like a wound.
'What will they be — become, I mean?' he said.
Their mother remarked, slicing a runner bean,
'They'll still be Jane
and Josephine.'

The English on Holiday

What is the matter with the English?
They sit so neat and tidy and silent,
in the dining-room at Seaview —
a thoughtfully considered place,
quiet, unobtrusive people running it
as smoothly as the cream
on the blackberry and apple pie —
sweet peas cut down to egg-cup size,
tablecloths next to Godliness,
and a view of the sea over the clipped-hedge wall,
and gulls swooping down, the waves crashing up.
Why are the English so dumb
over the grapefruit segments?
Straight up and down they sit, chewing.
Father, Mother, and Tobias in white socks.
Tobias is nine and flicks his eyes back and forth,
between courses, between parents.
Father is telling him facts under his breath,
while Mother looks down.
The sea soars reckless round the coast.
Why are the English so hushed over the triangles of
toast?

They are from Surrey and London and Bucks,
and they worry about A levels and what grade?
Mother is bright-eyed and blushing, tucking
abstemiously into the marmalade.

The A level candidates are up on the campsite
above the village, drunk, rowdy, flinging their noise
across the cowpats,
they are not at Seaview any more,
happily for their parents.

Later, though, a few years and they will come
down from the field with their white-socked children,
back into the dining-room at Seaview.

Why are the English so silent
framed in flowered chintz,
over their coffee and after dinner mints?

Leaflets

The leaflet has replaced the helping hand,
the helping hand is now a pile
of pamphlets saying where to go,
and when you get there they don't know.
They don't show mercy, that's no fun,
they tell you what you haven't done,
and pass you down the corridor
to other sorts of places,
where other people look and make
other sorts of faces.

And when you say you're penniless and homeless
and you've got a piece of red tape in your eye
and you've got a pain from reading piles of leaflets,
and the small print makes you cry,
and you're wearing thirteen pamphlets
'cos you can't afford a frock,
they say you should have noticed
that they close at four o'clock.

This earth that should be heaven and more
is now Form PP54.

The March of Progress

This plastic film
is dangerous —
suddenly after all these years
the experts say.
But wait —
in order to allay our fears and cheer us up
here's what to do about it:
put the food into a bowl
and cover it with a saucer . . .
Well, I never did! Oh my!
The March of Progress.
I can see my mother
putting that Susie Cooper plate
on top of a half-eaten jelly
in that orange and green fruit bowl,
I can see her quite clearly
and that was 1938.

The Lonely Widows' Club

Shirley knew it by heart,
what Mrs Pim-Brady had said:
'Do come along, do, to the lonely widows' club,
the first Monday in every month.'
She'd had a month to learn it,
she'd rehearsed it every night in bed —
the first Monday in every month.

And other widows would be there
and widowers, she hoped.
Her Kenneth wouldn't mind,
he wasn't there to mind,
he was dead.
There wasn't anyone to mind if she went out
the first Monday in every month.

It took her a month to get there, in her head,
ever since that woman on the phone,
she'd been alone
getting there.
It took her nearly an hour to walk there in her best dress,
raspberry gloss dry on her lips,
her stump of black-grey hair
held back with kirby grips.

She was late — 'There's a bus strike!' she told them —
they hadn't noticed with their cars.
The room was not festive,

no flowers, no gramophone, no bars,
nobody spoke to her, except the clock.
She smiled to detract from the uneven hem of her best
   frock.
When she saw the size twelve silk fluting gracefully down
to Mrs Pim-Brady's mid-calf
she smiled and let loose a silly laugh.
Plonking her size eighteen against the wall
she bent forward, offering a rough red hand.
'Have I come to the wrong hall?'
But Mrs Pim-Brady's hands were quite white and milky,
busy with criticism, privileged and silky.

The room was a cloakroom really,
shiny green chairs lined up opposite each other;
there was a piano singing nothing, polished and cold,
Shirl said she was new, she felt old.
Mrs Pim-Brady came noiselessly with a notebook and
   asked her name.
'Shirl!' she shouted. She meant to whisper
but she was full of shout.
She wanted to go then, to waddle out.
You could have heard a pin drop, she *did* hear a pin drop.
Some stony woman in pink
had brought her smocking to show them —
no one heard Shirl's spirits sink.
She was perched along with the others,
her hot thighs stuck to the shiny green.

Drips of sweat started the long journey to her bunions.
'Onions,' the smocking lady announced,
'you can dye your own linen with onion skins.'
The smocking lady didn't show them how to smock,
she told them that she could smock and she told them off
for not smocking.

Later, the widows got tired of her once she'd got on to
    dyeing,
dyeing linen in old bread bins with plant juice.
Nobody spoke to Shirl.

Ticked off with looks and very late, a jolly widow came
with a friend who was divorced, but she wasn't put in the
    book,
they didn't ask *her* name.
They got tea next and a biscuit
as soon as Mrs Pim-Brady gave the sign.
Shirl said: 'What a nice strong cup!'
but nobody took her up.
The widows whispered between sips and pain
and Mrs Pim-Brady discussed the next Monday in every
    month
and should it be smocking again?
The jolly widow, who was new too, was looking round
    dangerously.
'Where are the widowers?' the jolly widow asked.
After the shocked silence had made Shirl hiccup,
'One came once,' was the truly tiny reply.
The jolly widow left then, when no widower came by.
'See you next month, then,' Shirl said.
'Not on your life!' the jolly widow sniffed,

'toffee-nosed lot, d'you want a lift?'
That was nice of her . . .

Shirl sat on the edge of her huge double bed
and she bounced up and down, up and down.
'So much,' she said, 'for going on the town,
for trying to get about a bit.'
She was angry, which was an improvement on lonely,
that was one thing that came out of it.

The Adventure

I've got an adventure in my pocket
but I block it with my fear,
and shopping lists
for nothing much,
such
is my fear.

I've got an adventure in my pocket
screaming to get out,
it's certainly a liability
carrying it about.

And yet I feel it stirring,
it's occurring, very nearly,
and I love it very dearly,
but I can't set out
today.

Prepared

I'm ready for the
unexpected;
I'm always ready for it,
heady for it.

What I'm not ready for,
steady for,
is the expected.

I spend my time
preparing for surprise.
Anything planned ahead
is so mountainous,
so icy,
so fiery,
and it has to be written down
in a diary,
where it sits
afraid to be missed.
Well, I know something it doesn't know,
as far as today's concerned
it doesn't exist.

Just This Once

However I select the words
and underline, and dot the 'i'
and cross the 't' —
it will not be
exactly how it happened.

However finely all are drawn,
protagonists and crowd
and you and me,
it will not be
exactly how it happened.
   The past is past,
   the cast
   disbanded,
   they set sail for farther shores
   and have already landed.
   So I'll not tell the tale
   and people may believe
   what suits them
   as they would have anyway,
   and only I need grieve.

Or shall I?
Just this once,
be brave,
behave —
I'll put my armour on
and with a jumble sale of words

chuck out your pro and con,
lead up and strike
a wound so deep
that you will weep,
you all will weep.
  No, they will only turn away
  and check their bank cards
  and their smiles
  and make me pay.

That I should walk alone
and no one heed my yelling
might be the punishment
for telling,
and this I could not bear,
I'm too alone already,
my heart still thumps too fast,
my hand is still not steady.

Gatecrasher

There was this well-behaved party,
'Oh, thank you,' said everybody
to the hostess and the host,
accepting paté
on slim little slivers of toast
with sliced olives,
and crystal goblets of wine,
it was a mine-
field for the clumsy.
Then all of a sudden
the door burst open
and a man fell into the velvety room.
'Wotcha, folks!' he bellowed, plonking his hat
onto a perfectly coiffured head, whereat
he swigged alcohol,
stuffed himself with food,
sang at the top of his voice,
grabbed a horrified woman,
kissed her and pinched her bum,
then all of a sudden he left
as suddenly as he'd come.
Said one appalled girl to her friend,
'Who was that *awful* man?
He's made poor Eleanor cry.'
'Oh, don't be silly,' replied her friend,
'he's all right really,
he's just shy.'

Morning

The night, the sleep
used up, all gone,
the dish scraped
every last scrap.
O Lord, that was the bit
I enjoyed the best,
you can keep the rest,
the critical blue window
and the optimistic clutter
of leaves.

Unforgiven

In my palms
I hold my thumbs,
In my ears a roll of drums,
Rifles raised
Blindfold tied
Order given
Sleep died.

Must another day begin?
Must I let the morning in?
To whom should I be now appealing
To stop the vulgar sun revealing
All the loathsome disarray
Left by a fickle yesterday?

The darkness when I went to bed
Shadowed where my heart had bled.
Why can't the sun for once ignore
The mess that sleep forgave me for?

Dreams

Let it not be said
in my hearing
that dreams
are meaning
something else.
They are themselves —
my holidays.
Do not translate them,
I speak the language,
I do not need
your Freudian
creed,
I am fluent in the language
of my own lovely, horrible
dreams.

Spoiling for a Fight

Should we
on this sunlit autumn day
with summer bedding plants
still on display
and the hills purpling
before dusk
and no word
but breath and bird,
should we
with starvation a good way off
and death not quite producing its wares
and bankruptcy hardly
crashing at the door
and food in our mouths and beds upstairs,
should we, dare we
be unhappy?
Oh yes, we can do that readily
with our mega-star egos
ready and oiled,
the present is easily spoiled
with want and can't and don't and shan't
and give me, and why?
It's all right for you but I
am sullen and cross and watery-eyed,
eternally dissatisfied,
and want and want and want and wanting
head-over-heels and change
re-style, re-vamp and rearrange . . .

In spite of a mild September,
in spite of a cloudless night,
we're spoiling it all, we're spoiling it all,
we're spoiling it all
for a fight.

Wouldn't that be Absurd?

How polite people are
to the very rich.
Wouldn't it be absurd
if the reverse
were true,
and the poorer people were
the more people smiled at them
and said 'thank you'
and 'where would you like to sit?
Are you sure you're
quite comfortable there, Sir, Madam?

Anything we can do for you?
Just say the word . . .'
Wouldn't that be absurd?
It would make better sense, though,
it might put paid to greed
and possibly the accumulation
of money.
Wouldn't that be funny?

I believe that there are other worlds,
friends rather than foes,
and possibly that's where
Jesus goes.

If I were he, and living here,
which heaven forfend,
I'd be desperate
for a friend.

Flats

They sold that
cumbersome red church
and turned it into flats.
Flats for the poor?
Flats for the homeless?
Flats for the elderly? No, no, no.
What does the board say? Oh,
it says: 'Luxury flats for sale,
seven sold, one alone
remaining
with sauna, jacuzzi,
porterage and entry phone.'

The Passing of the Telegram

I wanted to alert my phoneless daughter —
a student, on a grant —
that a later train than first advised
would contain an aged aunt.
The man at British Telecom was useless,
I put the phone down with a slam,
he said the only thing to do
was to send a gorillagram.

I had to send some furry ape
to Newcastle upon Tyne
to read the following message:
Aunt Win arriving sixteen forty-nine.

The Firstborn Speaks

I don't mind that weeny baby,
but I wish they'd leave it alone,
and shut up about it being so sweet,
it hasn't done anything yet,
and I have,
I can get my socks on, on my own.

I'm nearly three
but I'd better hold the pram handle
very tightly
in case they forget about me.

The way they talk to that baby,
it's a complete waste of time,
it doesn't understand,
it hasn't done anything yet
and I have,
I can get the top off the toothpaste
and I can sing and run and hop
and run and hop and run
and climb.

Snails

I'm very angry with those snails,
They've eaten my mesembryanthemum,
I didn't ask those snails to come.

I'm very angry with those snails
In spite of their beautiful, silvery trails.
They've munched the glory out of my garden,
The succulent stems and the brilliant pink.

Said the snails: 'We weren't looking for visual pleasure,
We were looking for food and drink.'

Defeat

I am shy with animals.
I admire them,
but I don't pretend
to understand their speech,
I admire the inbuilt survival kit
of a bird or a mouse
but there's an end
to it.
A proper, adoring, maternal pet owner
I am not —
leads and chains and hutches,
pens, collars and cages,
they're not my bag
however the cats lick
and the dogs wag.
It feels undignified, patronising,
they seem to be sizing
me up —
and finding me wanting, which I am, I agree.
So I do not want to own an animal,
or for that matter for an animal to own me.
I admire animals —
dogs, cats, guinea pigs, hamsters, rats, mice
have all lived with me and my family
at one time or another,
but I cannot, will not be their mother.

I cannot take a free creature
and call it my own.

A bear may mate with another bear
but he's hardly likely to insult a dog
with a rubber bone.

Fact is I do not feel confident enough
of myself or my own breed,
an elephant may breed with another elephant
but he's hardly likely to keep
a badger on a lead.

Cowardice

I swallowed, silent, at the devil,
he drove victorious away,
instead I chose the innocent to shout at
all the following day,
until my children slipped upstairs
nearer to God than I,
nothing had they done but witness
cowardice rage by.

※※※※※※※※※※※※※※※※※※

Wrong Answers

I recall every silence
we have not broken,
I recall every meeting,
every parting,
every nothing —
but I could never add,
I never mastered sums,
my answers were always different
from the others.

Bent over the list of hours
I've spent with you
I come up with the same answer,
do I do too much multiplication?
Should I not divide, subtract,
be mean, be truthful?
Could do better.

I cannot,
the answer is always the same.

If you do not love me
then I am certifiable
which I have always thought
on the cards.
If what I feel from you
is not love
then I am past saving.

Or is it that my love
for you
is so great
that
having nowhere to go
It binds me falsely?

Light

I've been turning on the lights too soon,
both in the morning and the afternoon,
I never see the stars by day,
nor day by moon.

I miss the coming and the going of the night,
I need half light to cool and rest my eyes,
I need a slope of twilight
and the sun's slow rise.

※※※※※※※※※※※※※※※※※※※※

Just in Case

I'm going to the sea for the weekend,
in a couple of days I'll be back,
so I'll just take my little brown suit and a blouse
and a beret and carry my mac.

But what if the house is a cold one,
the house where I'm going to stay,
no fires after April, no hot drinks at night
and the windows wide open all day?
I'd better take one — no, *two* cardys
and my long tartan scarf for my head,
and my chaste new pyjamas in case they decide
to bring me my breakfast in bed.
And what about church on the Sunday?
I could wear my beret and suit,
but if it were sunny, it would be a chance
to wear my straw hat with the fruit.
I can't wear my little brown suit, though,
not with the straw with the fruit,
so I'll just take a silk dress to go with the straw
and a silk scarf to go with the suit.
I'll just take my jeans and that jumper
in case we go out in a car,
and my Guernsey in case we go out in a boat
and d'you know where my swimming things are?

D'you think I should take that black velvet
in case they've booked seats for a play?

And is it still usual to take your own towel
when you go somewhere to stay?
I had thought of just taking slippers,
but they do look disgustingly old,
I'd better take best shoes and sandals and boots
for the church and the heat and the cold.

I daren't go without my umbrella
in case I'm dressed up and it rains;
I'm bound to need socks and my wellies
for walking down long muddy lanes.

I'd rather not take my old dressing-gown,
it is such a business to pack,
but 'spose they have breakfast before they get dressed
I'd have to have mine in my mac.

I'm going to the sea for the weekend,
in a couple of days I'll be back,
so I'll just take my little brown suit and a blouse,
    two cardys, my long tartan scarf,
    my chaste new pyjamas,
    my straw hat with the fruit,
    my silk dress, my silk scarf,
    my jeans, that jumper,
    my Guernsey, my swimming things,
    my black velvet, my towel, my

        slippers (no one need see them)
        my sandals, my boots, my
        umbrella, my socks, my wellies,
        my dressing-gown, no, not
        my dressing-gown, OK my
        dressing-gown
and a beret and carry my mac.